Journey into Imagination
A History of Blackgang Chine

Copyright © 2015 by Joanne Thornton

All rights reserved. This book or any portion thereof may not be reproduced or used in any manner whatsoever without the express written permission of the publisher except for the use of brief quotations in a book review or scholarly journal.

First Printing: 2015

ISBN 978-1511898096

Joanne Thornton
34 Sunset Close
Freshwater, Isle of Wight, PO40 9JP

jothornton@btinternet.com

**Journey into Imagination;
A History of Blackgang Chine**

Joanne Thornton

Joanne Thornton
2015

Journey into Imagination

Acknowledgements

I would like to thank my family for their continued support and help in this project. I would also like to thank Alexander Dabell and the Blackgang team for their help and for the use of the Blackgang archive material. In addition, I would like to thank Simon Dabell for his time and for the information and photographs he has contributed. In addition, I would like to thank Brian Stotesbury for his contributions on the history of Blackgang.

Contents

Blackgang Chine through time   p8

A brief history of Blackgang Chine
and its surrounding area   p25

Blackgang Chine as a land of imagination   p33

Blackgang Chine events   p116

Conclusion   p127

Journey into Imagination

Blackgang Chine through time.

Blackgang Chine has been seen by many as a wonderland remembered fondly from childhood. This book sets out to give a brief history of the park and its attractions, in addition to providing photographs of some of the most popular attractions that have appeared at the park.

The Dabell family have steered the Blackgang experience through five generations and built up a tourist attraction, which started as a Victorian scenic landmark; their ingenuity and spin have played a large part in this story.

The Blackgang story begins with a young boy named Alexander Dabell. He had fled to the Island as a small boy with his family to escape the Luddite attacks up in Nottingham. The Luddites were groups of artisan textile workers who were protesting against the newly developed machines. These machines were designed to enable unskilled low waged workers to produce textiles at a faster pace than the skilled cottage workers. Some of the protesters took part in riots and set fire to the new machines. The Dabell family being lace makers had turned away from the traditional cottage industry and bought into factory style lace making; this made them prime targets for the Luddite protesters. Alexander's father set up a lace making factory in Newport, where Alexander worked once he was 13 years of age. His mother started a school, teaching the young children lace making skills. However, once Alexander turned 18/19 he decided that his future lay in retail and went up to London to learn this trade. Once he had served his apprenticeship, he returned to the Isle of Wight and set up a shop in Sandown selling homewares, lace and soft furnishings. The 1841 census shows that Alexander was living in the High street in Newport as a

Hairdresser, his wife Charlotte was a Milliner. He was also living with his sister Esther who was a Fruitier. In addition his father William, a Lace Maker and his mother Martha are also listed as living at the same address. Alexander sold hair gels as well as practicing hairdressing and having his soft furnishings business. His shop was so successful, that he opened more in Shanklin and Newport. Alexander became such a successful Island businessman. that he sold his name to prospective public house owners, to enable them to get licensed; as in the Victorian era, you had to be a well off businessman to be able to obtain a license to sell alcohol. Therefore Alexander Dabell saw his name over 30 + pub doors throughout the Island! One such man who needed this service was a W. Jacobs who happened to own land at Blackgang including the Chine. Mr Jacobs had decided to capitalize on the newly opened Sandrock spring located between Niton and Blackgang, by building the Blackgang Hotel. He then asked Alexander to be the licensee for this hotel.

The Blackgang Hotel

Journey into Imagination

This description details what the Blackgang Hotel was like to visitors:

*' The grounds are beautifully laid out with lawns and beds of flowers, and from these lawns, one has a splendid view of the Channel and the island's bays down to the Needles.
There is also a delightful conservatory which faces due south, where Mr Cotton grows the most splendid geraniums. It is comfortable; the staff courteous, there is splendid scenery and good liquor abounds at the Blackgang Hotel. '*

The Dining room of the Blackgang Hotel

An advert in Punch magazine for Kohler electricity, advertises that Blackgang Hotel was a well-known hotel and that it was one of the first places in the country to have Kohler's automatic electric plant system, which gave electric at the turn of a switch rather than using storage batteries.

Another event that occurred at this time to add to the visitor numbers to the Blackgang area was the wreck of the Clarendon. In 1836, this ship was wrecked just off the Blackgang shoreline. It was not the first ship nor was it the last to be wrecked there, however what brought it to everyone's attention was the passengers on board; An Admiral's daughter and a prominent business man who both perished. This wreck made the national newspapers and people came in coach loads to see the area where the ship had gone down. Alexander noticed this increase in visitors to the area, and as William Jacobs opened his hotel in 1837, Alexander asked him if he could lease some of the land. It is told that William agreed that he would lease Alexander the land up to as far as he could throw a stone! Whether he threw a stone or not, this is the start of Blackgang Chine being in the possession of the Dabell family.
In 1841/42 Alexander began to build the pathways down the Chine. At the top he built a retail shop, selling the same merchandise as his other shops, mostly homewares, soft furnishings, lace etc.
This may seem unusual to us, as most shops in tourist attractions today sell trinkets, and souvenirs so we can remember our visit. However, in the Victorian period, it would not have been at all unusual to the visitors at Blackgang Chine to have brought lace and Homewares to take back home.

Journey into Imagination

These very early pictures show how the Chine looked in the mid 1800s. In the left hand picture the waterfall and lanterns to light the pathways are clearly visible.

Early mid 1800 pictures of the Chine.

The first visitors came to the Chine in 1842, and Alexander was so successful in his first two years that he was able to buy the land from William Jacobs. Alexander noticed that due to the steep nature of the Chine, many visitors were getting tired by the time they reached the bottom, in addition, many of the visitors were wealthy and the women in particular had a job getting up and down all the steep steps in the Chine, especially in corsets and huge dresses which were the fashion in the Victorian period. Therefore he decided to build a verandah selling food and drink at the base of the Chine.

In 1846 the entrance price was 6d (2 1/2p). This was quite a lot of money in those days, especially to visit a garden, so Alexander made the entrance price free to those who spent a shilling (5p) in the shop. In order to let the people on the gate know who was to pay and who got in free, Alexander devised a special system for wrapping the gifts. If your gifts were wrapped in white paper, then they were worth under a shilling and you had to pay to get in; if they were wrapped in purple paper, you had bought items for more than a shilling and could go in for free

The old entrance to the Chine.

Journey into Imagination

In 1843, Alexander Dabell seized the chance to purchase from an auction, a whale that had become stranded on the Island beaches. It had come in at Gurnard, possibly coming free from a whaling ship coming past the Island. The Admiralty decided to place the whale in an auction, and Alexander was the only person who bid for it! He sold off the whale's blubber, and bleached the bones, before numbering them and dismantling them. They were then brought by horse and cart to Blackgang and re-erected in a tin house that Alexander had made for them. This was called the Whale house; He then opened a gift bazaar around the whale to further enhance his growing enterprise.

A whale on the beach.

The bazaar inside the whale's skeleton

The bazaar sold ceramics and homewares, offering for sale giftware from more than 25 different countries.

Gift bazaar

Journey into Imagination

By the 1880s Alexander had decided to add an exhibition of shipwrecks that had occurred along the Island's southern coastline, so he went around the local villages asking if anyone had any artifacts from these shipwrecks that he could add to the exhibition. However, he came away empty handed. Not to be deterred, he went round again, this time offering 3p for any items, needless to say he ended up with plenty of artifacts to display in his new shipwreck museum. In the late 1890s a smaller whale washed up on the south western shores of the Island, and this was also purchased to be displayed at the Chine. Unlike the larger whale, this whale was placed on a stand and positioned outside. Unfortunately this meant that the bones eventually fell to pieces due to the constant battering by the wind and rain coming off the channel. As a consequence the whale was dismantled in the 1960s.

Smaller of the whales, once positioned outside.

Tours were made to Blackgang Chine on a regular basis, In the 1900s, people joined organized tours to the Chine in a horse and cart.

Charles Dabell, one of Alexander's sons had a horse and coach service which ran twice a day from Blackgang via Niton to Newport leaving at 9.30 am and being back in time for lunch.

Coach such as the one taking people to and from the Chine.

These coaches were the first organized tourist tours for the Victorian tourists now flocking to the Island for their holidays. Most were wealthy Ladies and Gentlemen, as can be seen by the grand style of the carriage.

Mr Barnes took over in 1900 and ran a two horse coach, followed by his son who ran the first motorized carrier service in 1920.

Arthur and Percy Sprake, were Chale carrier owners; they received lots of work transporting goods to and from the Chine Bazaar. Their most unusual transportation was of a 'baby' elephant in the 1950s. At this time it was popular for people to want their photos

Journey into Imagination

taken with a stuffed animal and several stuffed animals were taken to the Chine over the years for this purpose. The elephant being one of them. This elephant caused quite a stir among the children of Newport as the carriers transported it from Newport railway station to Blackgang Chine!

By the 1920's a Charabanc was a more common sight taking tourists to the Chine. The name comes from the French 'Char a banc' meaning carriage with wooden benches. They normally had a large canvas folding hood. These were pretty basic vehicles, which were noisy, uncomfortable and often poorly upholstered, hence they were only usually used for short trips. As more working class people came on holiday due to the Factory Acts giving workers the right to holidays and time off work; tourism on the Island continued to boom, with bank holidays now given to the working classes, this meant day trips were possible, and many hundreds arrived on the Island piers in the paddle-steamers, which were a common mode of transport early in the 20th century. Day trips rather than actual weeks holidays were more common for the working classes who could usually only afford to go away for a day. It was not till the late 1960s that a weeks holiday had become the norm.

The popular charabanc with the hood down.

Charabancs were not only used by tourists, many islanders used them for day trips out. One account from a West Wight Sunday school tells of the Sunday school children having a trip over to Blackgang Chine as a treat in the 1920s.

Adverts in local newspapers such as the Isle of Wight County Press advertised various tours to popular Island attractions and places of interest, with pick up times and different options for the many visitors arriving, particularly during the summer months.

Journey into Imagination

VENTNOR, I. of W.

CRINAGE'S MOTOR COACH TOURS OF THE ISLE OF WIGHT

BOOKING OFFICE: Elizabeth House (Top of Cascade)

TOUR 1.—ROUND THE ISLAND.
Every Wednesday, departing from Elizabeth House at **10.30** a.m.

TOUR 2.—ALUM BAY AND THE NEEDLES.
On Monday, Wednesday, and Saturday, at **2.15** p.m., from Elizabeth House.

TOUR 3.—OSBORNE HOUSE AND RYDE.
On Tuesday and Friday, from Elizabeth House, at **2.15** p.m.

TOUR 4.—BLACKGANG CHINE AND CARISBROOKE CASTLE.
Every Thursday, from Elizabeth House, at **2.15** p.m.

TOUR 5.—BLACKGANG CHINE.
Every Afternoon, from Elizabeth House, at **3.15**.

Telephone 168.   *PRIVATE CARS FOR HIRE.*

Advert detailing tours to the Chine

It was not just wealthy gentlemen and women and the working classes that enjoyed trips to the Island for their holidays, but Royalty too!

Queen Mary was a regular visitor to Blackgang Chine; she accompanied her husband to the island and liked to wander around the Chine while he was busy racing his yacht in Cowes. One famous story relating to one of the Queen's many visits is that one day she was walking under the whale skeleton, and as she did so, part of the skeleton knocked off her hat! Needless to say, the offending part of the whale's bone was sawn off, while Mr Bruce Dabell, the manager at the time apologized profusely! If you walk under the skeleton today, you can still see where the offending part of the bone was hacksawed off.

Queen Mary on one of her many visits to the Chine.

Queen Mary usually purchased gifts in the Blackgang bazaar, which would be packed in her Majesty's own case with a Royal coat of arms on it. The Sprake brother's carrier service was often used to transport her purchases to the Royal yacht in Cowes.

Alexander was an ardent Baptist and he arranged for a woman Baptist preacher to have a spot, where she set up a tent at the Chine so she could preach to the visitors.

Journey into Imagination

He had the tin tabernacle at Chale built for her.

The Tin Tabernacle, now Christ Church in Chale

In the 1890's Walter, Alexander's son, who had taken over the running of the Chine from his father, had a stone version built at the entrance to the Chine, this later became the tearooms, but was originally a Baptist chapel complete with baptismal pool. The wooden pulpit reached the full height of the building.

The Mission Hall was not just used as a place of worship; the Blackgang Lifesaving apparatus company also used it as their meeting place. The lifesaving rocket crew were pivotal in many of the rescues that took place on the Blackgang coastline. These line-carrying rockets were fired over the stranded vessel to enable the heavy hawser to be hauled out, on which runs the breeches buoy. An example of a rescue is the wreck of the Wheatfield in 1882. This was a steamship on its way to New York. The crew managed to get in life rafts and get to safety, the Blackgang Lifesaving Apparatus Co, proceeded to try and fire a line over the ship.

However, the rocket was erratic, and turned soon after leaving the machine, heading back toward land. The ship soon broke up. This goes to show just how hard a job it was for the life savers in a very difficult area of shoreline.

Other shipwrecks where the crew were saved by the Blackgang Lifesaving Apparatus were the Capable in 1930, The Britisher in 1939, the Hope in 1948, and the Volkerak in 1951.

The Blackgang team attempting a rescue

Journey into Imagination

Alexnader Dabell died in 1898, his son Walter succeeding him, and his son Bruce after that. Bruce saw action in World War 1 and became injured by getting shrapnel in his leg, so he was sent to Netley Hospital to recover and fell in love with his nurse, who he married, and brought back to the Chine to help run it with him.

The portraits below show Bruce Dabell. and his grandfather Alexander Dabell.

Bruce Dabell   Alexander Dabell

A brief history of Blackgang Chine and its surrounding area

Blackgang and the surrounding coastline has long been site of shipwrecks. One of the most famous ships to be wrecked in the area, and the one responsible for the building of the Chantry on the summit of St Catherine's down is the St Mary. It was 1314 and a stormy night when this ship, the St Mary, which was laden with white wine from the Duchy of Aquitaine and heading for the monastery of Livers in Picardy was wrecked off the coast of Blackgang. The wine was washed ashore and claimed by the local lord of the manor, Walter De Godeton. This was a huge mistake on Walter's part; the wine belonging to the church meant that they took him through the law courts to get it back. He was even threatened with excommunication by the Pope! Walter was ordered to build a lighthouse on St Catherine's down to help warn ships of the dangerous coastline. He also had to build accommodation for a priest and assign him rents so he could sing masses for the souls of those lost at sea. For over 200 years a monk kept a lamp burning in the lighthouse until Henry VIII dissolved the monasteries. The nave has long since vanished but the tower still stands today as the 'Pepperpot' It was said that the monk was so unhappy that the chantry was dissolved that he set a curse on the land to make it slip into the sea!

'I curse the hell and I curse the strand, I curse the ground whereon I stand. Nor flowers nor fruit on this earth shall bear, but all shall be dark, and waste and bare. Nor shall the earth give footing dry, to beasts that walk or birds that fly. But a poisonous stream shall run to the sea bitter to taste and bloody to see.
(From Tales and Legends of the Isle of Wight; Abraham Elder 1839)

Journey into Imagination

St Catherine's Oratory

There was no other lighthouse after the Chantry was dissolved until a serious wreck off Blackgang brought about the building of St Catherine's lighthouse in Niton. This wreck was that of the Clarendon. It was 11th October 1836, when this ship was wrecked, and nearly all its crew were lost. The ship was smashed to pieces at the foot of the cliff, and those aboard drowned or killed by the falling timbers. The bodies were washed ashore, and many buried in Chale churchyard. The timbers were used locally in buildings. A contemporary account of the Clarendon tragedy tells how the ship struck the bottom of the Chine and by the time most of the Chale villagers had got to the bay, the ship had been driven to pieces by the waves pushing her onto the rocks. A fisherman, John Wheeler called to those on board to jump as this was their only chance. Only three were saved in the end, as the falling timbers crushed people in the water, and others got sucked under by the large waves. The Wheeler family became local heroes, and a life-saving team was created to help victims of shipwrecks.

The tragic loss of life stuck in the memories of all in the village, and prompted the official response of the building of the lighthouse at St Catherine's point in a bid to try and prevent further such tragedies in the future.

An etching of the Clarendon wreck.

Another wreck of interest to many local residents is the possible wreck of a Spanish treasure ship in 1702. A fleet carrying vast amounts of treasure was captured in Vigo bay by the Dutch and the English, but when returning home, the English fleet got separated by a storm in the channel. Of the six ships captured by the English only four seem to have been credited with returning. There may therefore have been two that never reached the English shore,

Journey into Imagination

getting wrecked perhaps in the storm. Does one lie off Blackgang's shoreline? The evidence for this being the large amounts of dollars that were picked up at Blackgang, the part of shore where people were finding them has been renamed 'Money Hole' In days gone past the old folk of Chale used to pick up these so called dollars by the handful, one man even claimed he found silver ingots. These dollars or 'pieces of eight' were all the same type of coin and dated 1701, giving credence to them being part of a wrecked Spanish treasure ship's hoard.

Example of the gold coins found on Blackgang beach

Examples of the coins found on Blackgang beach

An account from 1856, describes the Chine as a semi-circular chasm in the cliff, a 75ft wall of deep blue clay streaked with horizontal strata of sandstone, which is hollowed by the descending stream into a gloomy recess, this is battered with a constant spray and is darkened by the aquatic lichens. The stream descending perpendicularly, contrasting its bright waters with the dark hues of the wall behind it. The ocean waves surge up at the foot of the cliff, sending their echoes into the gloomy hollow. It is this haunting beauty that in part led Alexander Dabell to decide to open it as a Victorian attraction.

Journey into Imagination

This etching is an early representation of the Chine

Alexander Dabell built pathways around the Chine and viewing platforms for the visitors to see the charming beauty of the area.

The Fragrant Minute is a poem that was written in 1935 by Wilhemina Stitch, a columnist in the Daily Mirror at the time. In this poem she describes the Chine as an unusual and most impressive sight! She claims that the best feature of the Chine is the observation peak from where a clear view of the needles and Dorset's coastline can be seen.

Early photo of the Chine

Nearby to Blackgang Chine was the Chalybeate spring that was discovered at a site between Niton and Blackgang. This spring was discovered by a surgeon called Thomas Wentworth back in 1808. He obtained a lease for the land when he had discovered that the water contained a powerful tonic. He excavated the spring head and had an arch built over it to protect it from landslides. By 1810, he had built a dispensary and the spring was listed in guides to watering places and spas. This draw of people to the Sandrock spring also led to more visitors for Blackgang, as many stayed at the Blackgang Hotel built by Mr Jacobs. The water was said to contain alum and iron, the name Chalybeate coming from Chalybes in Asia Minor, renowned for its iron workers.

This spring was aptly named as the water was said to contain 41 grains of iron sulphide per pint, the brown coloured water was a reputed cure for diarrhea, dysentery and various nervous ailments.

Journey into Imagination

It was said the Queen Victoria had visited the spring, staying at the Sandrock Hotel, whence giving it the name Royal Sandrock Hotel. The spring was destroyed by a landslip in 1958.

Etching drawn by Brannon shows Sandrock cottage and the spring in the mid-19th century.

Blackgang Chine as the 'Land of Imagination.'

Many of the attractions that can now be seen at Blackgang were built in the 1950s, 1960s and 1970s. However, the earliest man made attractions date from the early 1930s.

In 1932, it was Bruce Dabell who first started to add the novel features to Blackgang Chine, creating the first 'theme park'.

The funny mirrors were originally installed in 1933, they show you 'how others see you'!

The ten original mirrors came from Paris. They were the first 'man made' attraction in the Chine.

The Hall of Mirrors

The famous Gnome garden goes back to 1934. The Gnome garden was created to raise £50 towards buying a car for the local district nurse, as Bruce's wife was a nurse he found this to be a good cause. The money was collected at the end of the season and was mostly

Journey into Imagination

in coppers. Being so heavy, the money was taken to the Newport banks via a carrier service, it was stored in tea chests in the back of the van! The money was usually divided up between the banks, there being such a large amount of coppers.

Gnomes were fashionable garden ornaments in Germany and Bruce had them made and brought over to make up the new attraction at the Chine.

Postcard of the gnome garden

  The garden gnome came into popularity in the 1930/40's, they are symbols of good luck, and they were originally used to give gardeners luck at night and to ward off thieves and pests. The gnome in folklore, lived underground and they were usually old men who guarded treasure. Therefore the gnome garden with its collection of money for charity connects well with the gnome in folklore. The gnome's garden today has copies of the original gnomes, but still collects for local charities.

The gnome garden in 2014

Gnome garden in the 1970s

gnome being repainted over winter

Journey into Imagination

The Chine also began to illuminate its gardens with hundreds of lights back in 1937, using their own generator, due to mains electric not yet being available to them, showing how cutting edge and unique the Chine was to even its early visitors. The fairy lights lit up the gorge for 4 weeks of August.

1960s poster advertising the Chine

The Chine was closed to the public in 1939 until 1947 due to the Second World War. Blackgang Chine was used as a training ground for Marine Commandoes, for 3 ½ years. This training was for them to become part of Churchill's secret army, and they were billeted in local homes, making them a part of the local community. The Marines were stationed aboard HMS Fidelity, under a civilian French commander. They set sail for the Far East on a mission to come behind enemy lines. However they never made it to their destination. HMS Fidelity suffered engine trouble and fell back from its convoy. This made it vulnerable and it was torpedoed by U Boat U435. There were only 10 survivors from the ships crew, and all 51 of the Marines died. There is a memorial to them in the churchyard at Chale.

It was in 1947, when Dick Dabell, joined the Blackgang team that many more features were developed to draw in more tourists and encourage imaginative play.
In the late 1950s, early 60s he took a trip to America to see the early Disney Park and Knotts Berry Farm, and used the idea of tableaux at Blackgang Chine to introduce unique themed areas to enhance the experience of the visitors to the Chine.
It was at this time that there was a dramatic change in the leisure industry, and there became a mass market for tourism, as people got over the war years and wanted to enjoy themselves on their holidays.
The park began its change into a more tourist orientated attraction. The Dabell family in keeping up with the needs of the visitors in the post war years started to add new attractions year by year to build up the now popular 'amusement' park. The maps of the park through the years give a good representation of just how much the park has evolved and changed over time, not just with the addition of attractions, but with the changing landscape due to cliff erosion, and the constant movement of existing attractions to safer, more stable areas within the park.

Journey into Imagination

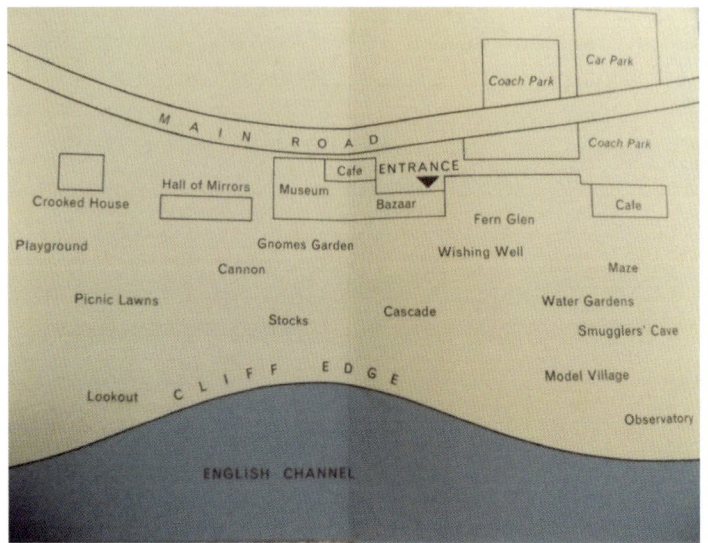

Early map from the late 1960s.

The next item to be added to the park by Dick Dabell was the model village, which was built in 1953, this consisted of a collection of scale models featuring many of the Isle of Wight's more famous buildings and attractions. Some of these models actually worked, such as the Yafford mill model which had a working water wheel and the clock tower on the Osborne house model which showed the correct time. The model of Whippingham church even had music from the organ playing, with occasional singing from the choir. Each model was located in its own setting, backed by flowers and shrubs, giving a more natural backdrop for the miniature scale models. Unfortunately the model village was removed after the landslip of 1994.

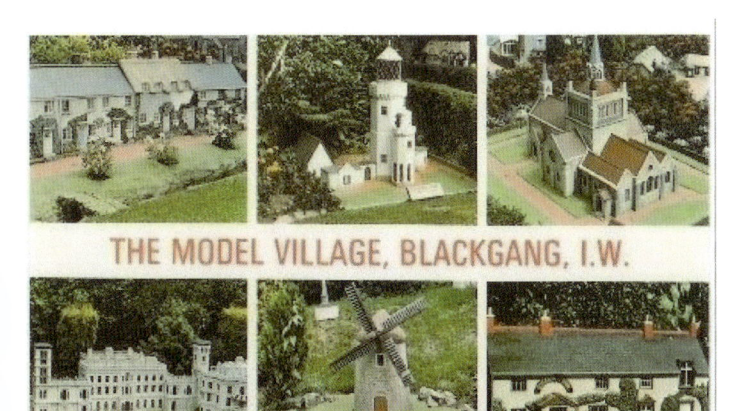

Postcard depicting various buildings in the model village

Early photo of the model village

Journey into Imagination

The smugglers cave was created in 1954. It depicts the wreck of the Clarendon at Blackgang in 1836. The Clarendon was driven ashore during a storm, and many that perished are buried in Chale. The smugglers cave is in the style of a cave with tunnels that create a winding pathway with scenes that depict an animated story of the shipwreck.

Entrance to the smugglers cave

Early smugglers cave exhibit

The water gardens were constructed between 1961-62. They are a series of pools, cascades and fountains in landscaped gardens, which were floodlit at night by underwater lighting. When the attraction first opened, the floodlighting consisted of colour changing floodlights under the water at the base of the fountains, which automatically faded from green, to blue to pink. The gardens were constructed out of wasteland, and designed to give a pleasing terraced aspect with the tumbling waterfalls, and three pools containing fountains. In all, over 400 tons of earth was excavated, 10,000 bricks were used, 235 tons of concrete, 55 tons of top soil and 45 tons of rockery stone. In addition, 1500 privet bushes were planted and 350 trees and shrubs, a massive undertaking! A 3 hp unit was used to circulate the water at 25,000 gallons per minute. The water gardens are still in existence today but with a slightly different layout to the original.

The illuminated water gardens

Journey into Imagination

Photograph of the early water garden design

The modern water garden design

Although the water gardens are still in their original positioning, the fountains have been replaced by waterfalls, and more unusual smoking barrels as landscaping features.

The maze was planted out in 1963, and still survives to this day. Mazes are a series of pathways designed to form a puzzle which must be solved in order to get out. Over 5000 bushes were used in its construction. Blackgang used to hold maze races, where people would try and find their way out of the maze in the quickest time possible. The maze also featured on Channel 4's Treasure Hunt series, with Anneka Rice getting lost in the maze.

As these two pictures show the maze has not changed much over the years.

An early photo of the maze

Journey into Imagination

Photo of the maze in 2014

Moby Dick's revenge was originally a walk through whale with aquariums displaying real fish. The whale is a 35ft long glass fibre structure. The sculpture is by John Baldwin of Design and Display Productions Ltd, and was constructed in his London Studio. Mr Dabell arranged for the whale to be taken from it's London Studio to the BBC Television centre and be constructed for the Blue Peter programme. The whale was then disassembled and transported to the Isle of Wight. It was originally sited in Nurseryland. The Isle of Wight County Press, reports the whale's arrival on 23rd March 1974.

Moby Dick being transported to Blackgang

Journey into Imagination

The whale arriving on a ferry

Today, the whale features as Moby Dick's revenge, where water jets squirt you on your way through.

The whale 2014

The crooked house was originally built in 1968, and is a full-scale model of a house except that its floors and rooms are crooked. It is based on the nursery rhyme of the crooked house. This rhyme is written on the walls as you travel round the house. The fun lies in trying to navigate your way along the uneven floors and wonky passageways. It still exists in the park today with very 1970s décor throughout.

There are even some stocks and pillories outside that you can try out for size! These were originally used for petty criminals, who would be held in them so villagers could throw rotten food at them as a form of punishment!

The crooked house 2014

Journey into Imagination

The kitchen of the crooked house

Adventureland

Adventureland was introduced in 1970, and not only consisted of play equipment, but also disused military vehicles, including an armored car and tanks, as well as old cranes, steam rollers , and a Ruston Bucyris digger, which children could climb on and play in. There was even a Bristol Bloodhound MkII Rocket, resting in its cradle, which was used by the RAF as a surface to air missile.

Space shuttle and armored cars

Steam rollers and various vehicles in Adventureland

Journey into Imagination

Crooked house and playground 1980s

Alongside the various tanks and other machinery, was traditional playground equipment, including a helter skelter slide, swings, and a roundabout

Playground in 1980s

Due to Dick having formed a close relationship with Pinewood studios, he purchased the space shuttle prop from the film 'The spaceman and King Arthur.' This was a 1979 Disney film, where a NASA spacecraft travels back in time to the kingdom of Camelot.

Model space shuttle arriving at the park

Journey into Imagination

Dick Dabell also purchased from Pinewood studios, a mockup of the James Bond submarine 'Neptune' from the film 'For your eyes only'

The submarine arriving at the park

The Dinosaur Zoo

The first 6 large dinosaurs were airlifted into the park during May of 1972, by a Wessex helicopter. They were made from glass fibre reinforced plastic, and mostly constructed to full scale except the largest which were to ½ scale.

The arrival featured on the Blue Peter programme at the time; this publicity really helped to put Blackgang on the map for tourism. The coupling of Kelloggs model dinosaurs in cereal packets and the new school curriculum which now included them, made Blackgang a popular choice for visitors to the Island now that they had the new dinosaur park. The other dinosaurs were put into position during the summer.

Postcard showing some of the dinosaur models

Journey into Imagination

Helicopter flying in the dinosaur models to the park

Helicopter carrying the dinosaur models into Blackgang.

Journey into Imagination

The dinosaurs situated in the Dinosaur zoo

The Mouth of Hell was located in Dinosaur land. Inside there are demons and once you enter you are supposed to exit only by the small hole in the centre or else be eternally damned! This could be from the Baptist leanings of the Dabells, and represent how Hell is easy to get into but hard to escape!

The Mouth of Hell 2014

Nursery Rhyme Land

This land opened in 1974, it depicts popular children's rhymes, including a lifesize house that Jack built, and an area with toadstool houses and the popular gnome on the toadstool which is repainted with the date each year; many visitors have their pictures with this gnome as a souvenir. The Fairy Castle which was first built in 1972, used to stand in Nursery Rhyme Land. It now stands in Fairyland. The Castle with its battlements and secret passages is based on a real castle in the mountains of Austria.

The fairy castle 2014

The fairy Castle later had a tableaux added inside depicting the story of Sleeping Beauty, surely a take on the famous Walt Disney Sleeping Beauty's Castle.

Journey into Imagination

Nursery Rhyme Land also contains a toadstool village, a singing tree which you can look inside to see elves all playing musical instruments and if you listen carefully at the doors and windows you can hear their tune! Furthermore children can immerse themselves in familiar rhymes, as they come to life in tableaux. They can see Humpty Dumpty on his wall, walk around the House that Jack built and climb through The Old Woman's Shoe! Hickory Dickery Dock's Clock used to have live mice inside it, but today they are just models.

Humpty Dumpty model 2014

Gnome and toadstool with date of current year

Old woman in the shoe, House that Jack built and little piggies

Journey into Imagination

Buffalo Creek

This land was created at the bottom of Blackgang Chine, down in the woods. Buffalo Creek was built in 1976 on land purchased by the Dabells; once the houses built there originally had become unstable and demolished. These houses were called the Southlands estate. Southlands house was built in the 1840s, and in 1865 purchased by Rev Dr Pusey. He renamed it the Foreign Mission House. There was a wooden annexe to the building which was occupied by a Lady Superior, several sisters of mercy, Princess Polama and some other Polynesian children from the Sandwich Islands, which are now known as Hawaii. These children had been brought over to England so they could be taught, but unfortunately it is believed they contracted TB and died at a young age. After Rev Pusey's death the house became a sanatorium. It was adapted to house up to 70 residents that required a change of scene and needed to convalesce in a quieter environment than an ordinary hotel could provide.

Southlands house

The Dabell family, having grown up at Blackgang used to run around the area playing Cowboys and Indians, so with the land now theirs, they thought it would be fun to build their own Cowboy town and Indian camp. With the help of Pinewood Studios, who designed and constructed all the buildings, a frontier town was born.

.Postcard of the original Buffalo Creek

The Blacksmith's forge had a horse being shod, while the saloon had the traditional 'western type' swinging doors for visitors to swagger through! There was a bank, being held up by a robber, and a Wells Fargo office with the telegraph operator waiting to send messages in Morse code.

Journey into Imagination

Stage coach and horses arriving at Blackgang

Panning for gold, where visitors could search for and find their own pieces of gold to take home.

The gold mine at Buffalo Creek

The Trappers cabin was set further in the woods and nearby was a model of a family of bears

Journey into Imagination

The train situated in Frontier land was commissioned by the Dabells to be made by Pinewood Studios.

The train arriving by lorry to Buffalo Creek

The train situated in Buffalo Creek

A fort was also build near to Buffalo Creek containing play equipment for children to play on. Fort Buffalo was opened in 1985, as a cavalry fort. The Fort was complete with canyon swings, rope bridges and tunnels, it was an exciting activity centre and soon became very popular. It was built from Lakeland logs overlooking Rocken End. Due to its remote location a helicopter had to be drafted in to aid in the building of the fort.

The Buffalo Creek frontier fort: Fort Buffalo

Journey into Imagination

Smugglerland

Smuggling was rife in the Isle of Wight, especially along the south coast. If there was ever a more suitable theme for a land at Blackgang then it would have to be this one! There was a coastguard watch station located at Blackgang to try and catch the smugglers as they came in with their goods. In the villages of Chale, Niton, and Whitwell there were many men and women involved in the smuggling trade. The ones who took the boats out were mainly fishermen, as they knew the treacherous coastline best. The shore crew were mainly farmers. The wives and children would also help in the concealing of the goods. One tale tells how when the revenue men came to call, the wife sat in the bed with tubs of brandy and a baby doll pretending to feed the baby. The revenue men satisfied that nothing was amiss left her in peace! Little did they know that they had just walked past the previous night's haul! Not only were houses used to hide smuggled goods, but also gardens, ditches in fields, secret hidey holes and coastal caves. The Smugglerland at Blackgang depicted the passageways and gives some idea of the secret hideouts used by the local people, by using the suspended bridges between the treehouses. There are tales of roofs in terraced houses having tunnels between them so that goods could travel from house to house unknown. Smugglerland had a galleon ship, along with connecting bridges suspended from model trees entering into the Smugglers Rest Inn.
Many unlicensed alehouses cropped up in the local area, selling illicit spirits to not only the working folk but often the gentry and clerics as well. In fact churches and graveyards were often used to conceal liquor tubs. The churchyard at Chale being one of the smuggler's hiding places!

Chale Church

The tower walkway in Smugglerland

Journey into Imagination

Once the land slip had occurred, the suspended bridges were removed and the ship moved further back.

The landslip in Smugglerland 1994

For years Smugglerland consisted of only a galleon ship, smugglers rest and cave, but in 2012, Smugglerland received a facelift, and became Pirate Cove. Another galleon ship was built and now there are two ships sitting opposite each other, both having water cannons on board to shoot each other, and enable visitors to have a 'pirate battle'.

Jungleland

In 1979, Jungleland was opened. This started in the woodland walk and consisted of many wild animals that children could sit upon and have their photograph with. There was even Tarzan up in the trees!

Crocodile in Jungleland

Jungleland gave children the opportunity to climb on and walk amongst models of animals that they may have only seen in picture books or perhaps a zoo. Travel abroad was very rare at this time and it gave children in the 1970s and 1980s a chance to imagine they were in the jungle, somewhere they were not likely to have the opportunity to visit

Journey into Imagination

Elephant arriving on a lorry to Blackgang

The 1980s

The 1980s saw a transition from the longer holidays taken in the times of the 'factory fortnight' to a surge in popularity of short breaks, as more parents both went to work, and it became harder to get periods of time off together.

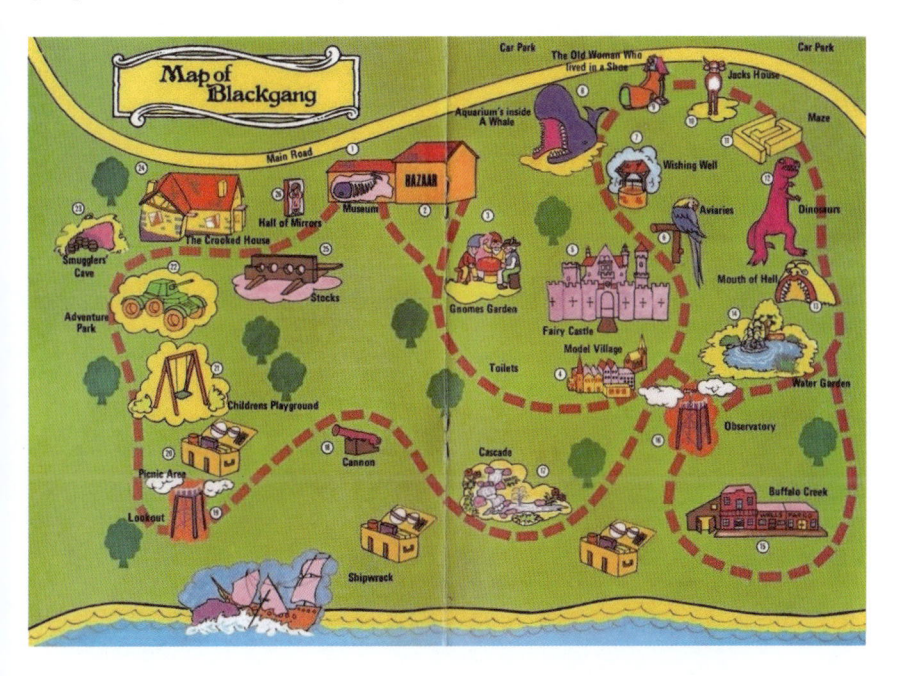

This map from the 1980s shows how the park has evolved since the 1969 map with a lot more attractions added over the previous decade.
In the year 1980 Mission control or the Lunar base as it was first called opened. It was described as "an exciting visual representation of a space vehicle's ground control centre complete with the 'space shuttle' ready for take-off outside"
This was located in Adventureland, amongst the model space craft.

Journey into Imagination

Mission control being built

Space shuttle situated next to Mission control.

The Ship Ashore Inn also opened its doors in 1980, after an extensive refurbishment programme. It is one of Blackgang's oldest buildings as it was once the taproom and stables to the hotel. It may once have been an unlicensed drinking house for the local residents back in the 17th century. It was certainly trading in the 1830s. The central gabled area contained the Taproom, with the wings on either side containing enough stabling for 20-30 horses. It was known as the Tap until 1963, when it changed its name to the Ship Ashore. The Victorian's would frequent the area to 'take the waters' and people came from all over to stay at Blackgang, and also to view the newly opened Chine.

It was also in 1980 when the smugglers cave received its revamp and the installation of the animated display of the Clarendon wreck.

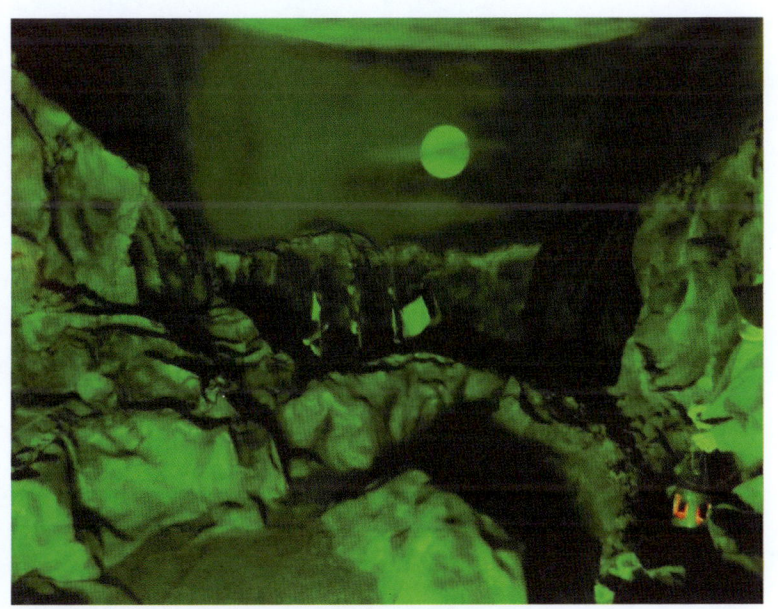

Animated display in the re-vamped smugglers cave

Journey into Imagination

The 1980s also saw the creation of the Blackgang sawmill attraction and St Catherine's Quay. The Blackgang sawmill exhibition opened in 1981.

The sawmill and world of Timber display

The Sawmill was constructed from a house called Crohana, which was originally a 17th century barn, then a coach house to St Catherine's hall, before being converted into a cottage. It displays a mill owner's kitchen and a bedroom, furnished in a typical Victorian tradition. There is a working water wheel, and the Sawmill tells the story of timber including the sawing and transporting of logs. In addition the craft of a wheelwright, fence maker, cooper and others are illustrated using life size figures. There is also a display showing early boatbuilding methods. In the Jan 9th 1981 edition of the Isle of Wight County Press, Mr S Dabell states that he is hoping that the museum will be entertaining and educational, and will show early 20th century woodwork methods and craft

St Catherine's Quay

St Catherine's Quay opened in 1984 and contains an Isle of Wight Ferry museum. It originally opened as a maritime exhibition set around a 19th century quay side.

It contained an exhibition of smuggling artifacts, and displays about the RNLI and the shipwrecks that the local area has seen over the years. A Liverpool class lifeboat called the Friendly Forester that was built on the Isle of Wight in 1953 is displayed at the quay. It is one of the last of its kind, and still shows the traditional pulling and sailing hull design.

The Friendly Forester

St Catherine's Quay later contained an exhibition on landslips in the area, and a coast exhibition containing information on Britain's coastline. The Dabells use the landslip exhibition to capitalize on

Journey into Imagination

their assets that are no longer there! By displaying information and photographs of the buildings and land that has disappeared into the sea. This attraction won a number of awards including the Carnegie Interpret Britain award.

St Catherine's Quay also contained an exhibition of the history of the IOW ferries. The engine of the Compton Castle paddle steamer was removed from where it docked in Cornwall and brought over to be displayed in St Catherine's Quay, in a room that was reconstructed as a paddle steamer engine room. The Compton Castle was built in 1914 and regularly visited the Island in her heyday. The paddle steamers used to dock at the Island piers, bringing loads of visitors to the Island.

Compton castle engine room reconstruction

The Compton castle in her heyday

The famous whale Skeleton is displayed in the Quay building, where visitors can walk through and even sit in a wishing chair that is positioned in the Whale's jaws. The wishing chair had a sign saying that it was lucky to wish inside a whale, as Jonah did and he got out! The whale skeleton is of a fin whale and is the biggest specimen ever found on the British Isles. A museum of smuggling artifacts were displayed around the whale skeleton, but today there is special light effects and information on whales surrounding the skeleton.

Journey into Imagination

Whale skeleton located in St Catherine's Quay

A major project of the building of a new entrance and giant 30ft smuggler was commenced in 1985 after planning permission was granted. There was a need for a new entrance as this area and some of the other attractions were threatened with erosion and needed to be relocated.

Old main entrance to the Chine

The main entrance and shop are now accessed by walking through the legs of the giant smuggler! A new road and a roundabout were also built at this time. The need for a new entrance was due to the constant erosion of the cliffs, not only was a new entrance built, but lots of the attractions were in need of re-siting. No new attractions were built for three years during the building phase. The Chine had lost 80ft of land in the years preceding the building of the new entrance, which was 3 times the normal erosion rate for the Chine. The new entrance is sited next to the old Blackgang Hotel, which today serves as offices and the main Chine restaurant.

Journey into Imagination

The 30ft smuggler being erected

At the official opening in April 1987, Mr Simon Dabell confirmed that in the last 2-3 years 100ft of cliff had been lost to erosion Among those present at the grand opening was the Island MP and the Mayor of the South Wight.

Official opening of new entrance in 1987

In May 1989, a landslip occurred at Blackgang Chine, this caused the closure of the Model Village and the Fairy Castle. A 40ft stretch of cliff had dropped about 8ft back and large cracks had appeared in the ground around the model village and fairy castle. All of the models that were threatened with slipping down the cliff were retrieved and the area was monitored for further slippage. However on the 12th May the chief engineer for the South Wight Borough Council detected further movement. Mr S Dabell, reassured visitors that the model village and Fairy Castle would either be re located at the end of the season, or new attractions would replace them. The Fairy Castle was relocated, but it was decided to not relocate the model village and to replace it with another attraction.

Journey into Imagination

In 1988, Orbiter V space ship simulator was installed at the park. However, It was scrapped after only a few years due to new regulations and the costs associated with keeping it running. The simulator showed a film of flying over the Isle of Wight, before shooting up into space and engaging in a battle with alien spacecraft, before eventually returning to the safety of Blackgang Chine. The Orbiter was originally called the Astro Glider by the manufacturer, but Blackgang rebranded it and recorded a new film.

It was advertised as a computer controlled sound and motion simulator, where visitors can experience a thrilling ride along the island coastline and a galactic attack from alien space fighters!

An Orbiter V passport could be purchased as a souvenir of your 'space flight'.

The orbiter being lowered into place

The Astro Glider before being re-branded as Orbiter V

Orbiter V Passport

Journey into Imagination

The 1990s

This decade saw the introduction of many new attractions, along with the demolition of some of the original features due to cliff erosion. The year 1993 was a landmark year for the park; marking its 150th anniversary. The character of Bron Brontosaurus was introduced in the early 1990s, it was created by David Bellamy. This character was followed by Bodger The Badger, and Connie The Fox. In addition to these characters, many new events were staged at the park. This decade also saw the introduction of rides, as the Dabell family brought the park into the modern era. The map from 1993 shows how the park had changed from the 1980s, although, this pre 1994 landslip map had changed dramatically by the end of the decade as Blackgang's layout moved in line with the coastal erosion, when the Cowboy town and the Snakes and Ladders had joined Rumpus Mansion across the road from the rest of the park.

Map of the park from 1993

The tearooms, which had once been the Baptist Mission Chapel complete with a Baptismal pool, had to be pulled down as the cliff eroded ever closer, making it unsafe. This was less than a year after the old entrance and whale house were pulled down.

However, there were many new ideas in the pipeline to replace the demolished and removed features. These new ideas included the iconic Snakes and Ladders board game, which was built to a giant size and came to life in the park in 1990. Originally this giant size board game was further down the cliff, but due to land slippage had to be moved to a higher location after 1994.

The game consists of giant slides as snakes and steps for the ladders, which children have to climb or slide according to the giant dial they spin at each platform.

Snakes and Ladders before its re-siting in 1995.

Journey into Imagination

Fantasyland

Another completely new land opened in 1991; Fantasyland. This new land saw the opening of The Weather Wizard, Licorice House, which smells of licorice! A parrot that talks back and there is a roaring dragon. There are also numerous toadstools for children to sit upon.

The Weather Wizard attraction displays animated scenes of the four seasons; spring, summer, autumn and winter. Spring shows flower girls, Summer has a honey bee display, Autumn has a pixie painting the leaves, and Winter shows ice monsters turning crystals to make snow. At the end a wizard tells the children about how he controls the weather!

The Weather Wizard attraction

The weather wizard

The Licorice House

Journey into Imagination

The dragon

The toadstools in Fantasyland

The Musical Pet Shop opened in 1992, with novel singing animals

The entrance to the pet shop

Meet a Tasmanian devil, horse, dog, cat, parrot, spiders, guinea pigs, a rabbit and a snake! All singing or dancing along to a Blackgang themed song!

Journey into Imagination

The interior of the pet shop

In 1993 the Dabells took steps to ensure that should Blackgang Chine eventually disappear into the sea, they would have some legacy of this imaginative fantasy park. By forming their company Vectis Ventures, they purchased the Robin Hill site. Presently the fiberglass figures from Jungle Land have moved to the Robin Hill site where they form part of the safari play area for children.

Rumpus Mansion

Rumpus Mansion opened in 1993. This was converted from a house where the Dabell family formerly lived, called Five Rocks. Inside this stone house are legends and folklore of the British Isles. From Ginny Green teeth to fairies and Cornish knockers, Meet the three witches, a ghost, a unicorn and dragon and even the Seelie

King and Queen.! The Seelie King and Queen head up the court of the light fairies, known for their light hearted attitude and for playing pranks on humans! So watch out when you exit from this unusual house incase fairy folk have decided to join you and hop in your bag!

Rumpus Mansion

The maid and the fairy sprites inside Rumpus mansion

Journey into Imagination

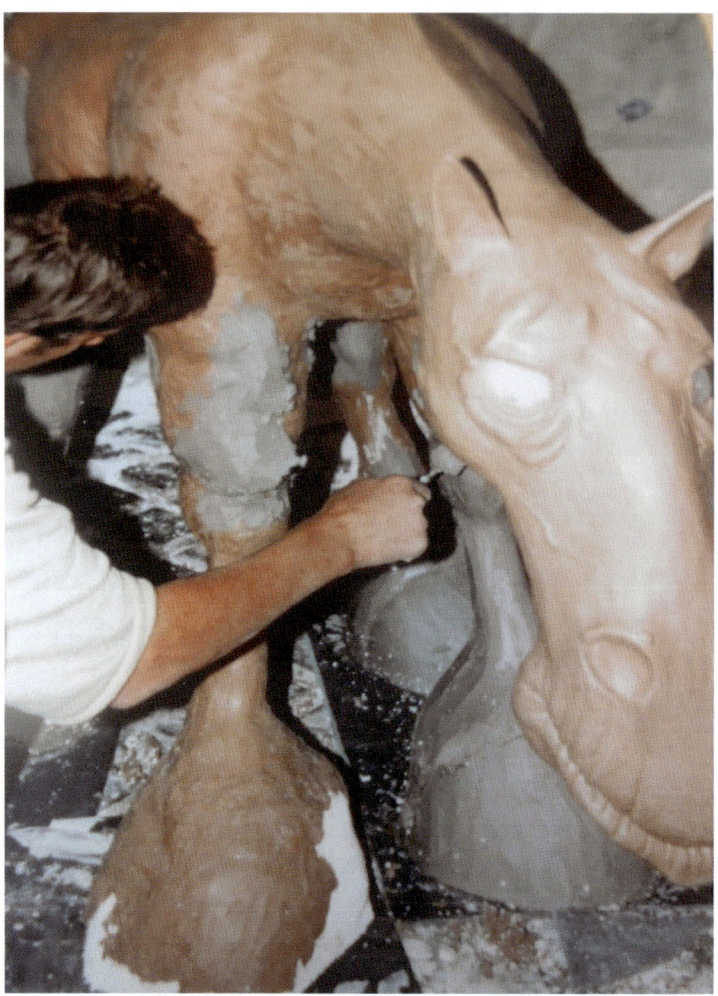

The unicorn being made for Rumpus mansion

In 1994, Blackgang suffered damage from a large landslip, however being as entrepreneurial as the Blackgang team are, they did not let this get in the way of creating new attractions for visitors. They decided to use their assets to their advantage, even if some of them were disappearing into the sea! Blackgang also displayed the media coverage of the slips.

Media coverage from the landslip

Another new attraction this year was a clock tower for Rumpus Mansion, located at the entrance to the bridge that links the lower area of the park to the upper area, where Frontierland was relocated. The clock tower cost the park £30,000; this had goblins popping in and out with the chimes. However, it was taken down after only a few years as it became unstable.

Journey into Imagination

The gatehouse, with goblins popping out!   Original design for the gatehouse

After being removed from the gatehouse, the goblins were reused in fairyland.

The Triassic Club

The Triassic club was opened following the landslip. This exclusive club for dinosaurs is built on the site of an old swimming pool. Here the sign tells how The land cracked and slipped away to reveal something strange indeed, this strange occurance was a dining club of dinosaurs. Visitors to the club can be weighed to determine which course they would be; Starter, main course or perhaps A'La Carte! Do not worry if you are vegetarian as Darwin the allosaurus does not like to eat them!

Darwin the Allosauraus

The waiter, ready to welcome you into the club

Journey into Imagination

Frontierland

Aside from these new attractions the Blackgang team were forced to make other changes. Buffalo Creek had to be closed, Snakes and Ladders was taken down, and part of Smugglerland had to be removed. These features were later re-located to higher land, and opened again in 1995.

The new cowboy town had many of the old buildings from Buffalo Creek which had been saved, but also had some new additions, including a funeral parlour, and mine, along with La Cantina, where cowboy style snacks are sold. A new Boot Hill was also erected, featuring some new headstones and a new Indian Camp, the three bears were relocated the new Frontierland. In addition, there was a new panning for gold area.

Frontierland

Fort Tortuga

In 1997 it was decided to build a £70,000 Pirate fort behind St Catherine's Quay, called Fort Tortuga. Features included an imposing skull and crossbones on the entrance, which one walked under to enter the fort. There were also rope walks, a tunnel crawl, helter skelter and a rope side. Children could also take part in a treasure hunt, where they went around the fort picking up clues to find Long John Silver's treasure. This replaced the cowboy fort which used to be down in Buffalo creek; when the Cowboy town was moved more inland after the landslip, there was no room for a separate fort, so a pirate fort was built instead.

Fort Tortuga

Journey into Imagination

In 1998, Blackgang saw the grand opening of Blackgang's first ride, the Water Force attraction. The giant water slides offer two open slides where children can race each other and the plug hole, a covered slide. The slides are 80ft long, and the boats travel at between 25 and 30 mph. This attraction cost approximately £30,000 to build.

The three water slides

The Spicey Girls opening the water force attraction

The grand opening saw a tribute band for the Spice girls, 'The Spicey Girls' arrive in a limousine with a police escort. They then proceeded to entertain the crowd with a 30 minute set of Spice Girls songs before trying out the slides for themselves!
One of the Blackgang team even dressed up as Queen Victoria for the event and succeeded in beating the Spicey Girls down the slide!

Journey into Imagination

2000 onwards

The new millennium saw Blackgang move into providing more rides and attractions with the advancing technologies and special effects that were now available. The park increasingly changed to adapt towards changing visitor expectations, as more tourist attractions emerged, and competition increased. In addition to the more traditional tableaux that Blackgang had become famous for, the Dabell family now started to add more thrill rides, and animatronic exhibits.

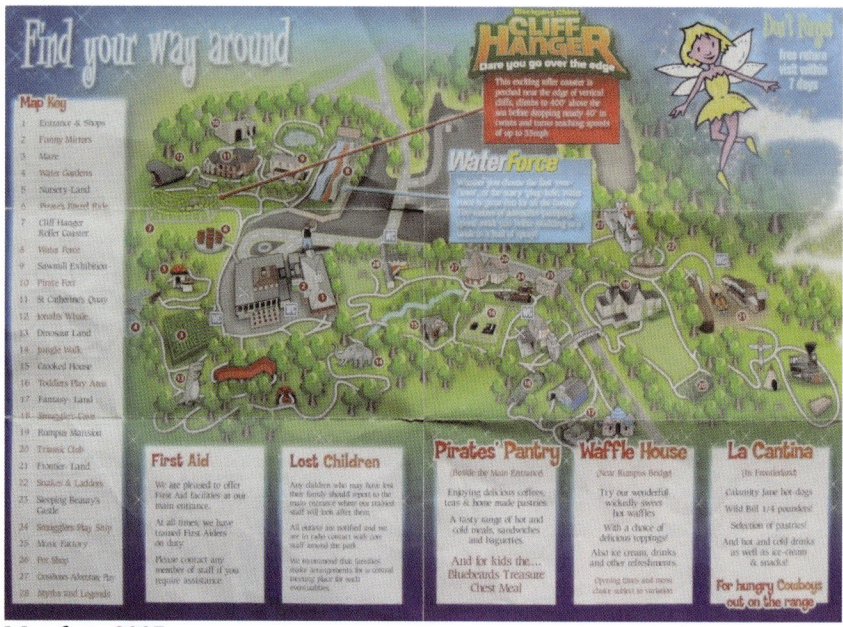

Map from 2007

In 2003 the Blackgang team was awaiting the delivery of the Tornado rollercoaster. This rollercoaster had a 200 metre long track, with a 9 metre drop, double spiral and camel backs. The planned grand opening was a VIP party of 160 guests, to celebrate the 160 year anniversary of the park. The rollercoaster failed Health and Safety assessments.
The Dabells launched a £1 million legal claim against the company that built the Tornado, Westech Ltd. Westech did not honour their agreement with Blackgang to provide a rollercoaster that could be used and then failed to honour the agreement to dismantle and remove the rollercoaster if it did not pass Health and Safety tests.

The first Tornado rollercoaster

In 2005 Blackgang Chine opened a new rollercoaster, The Cliffhanger. This rollercoaster was built by I.E. Park, an Italian company. The Cliffhanger cost £590,000, and climbs up 38 feet which drops to a twisted track and a helix.

Journey into Imagination

The Cliff hanger rollercoaster

The junior pirate barrels ride followed the opening of the rollercoaster, offering a ride for younger children in 2006. This is a pirate take on the classic teacup ride.

The Pirate Barrels ride

As the land settled, the Blackgang team decided to build a giant bug walk leading up from the dinosaur area. On the way up to the bugs, you pass through the butterfly walk, displaying models of various butterfly species. At the top of the butterfly walk there is a giant potting shed, complete with a giant allotment and vegetables next to a bench where two gnomes are sitting. These gnomes will even chat away when you sit down!

The giant potting shed and allotment garden

Journey into Imagination

The talking gnome bench

Giant bugs on the bug walk

In 2010, a Disappearing Village exhibition and Britain's Coast exhibition opened in St Catherine's Quay. This exhibition detailed the landslips in the Blackgang area. Originally Blackgang village was a collection of Victorian villas and Fishermans cottages looking over the ¾ mile long, 400ft deep Chine gorge. However, over the last 150 years almost ¾ mile of coastline has fallen into the sea at Blackgang and the 'Disappearing Village' detailed these slips.
There was also the new attraction called 'Wight Experience' which is an aerial film of the Islands beauty and heritage. Furthermore, the Ship Ashore opened as a tearooms alongside a chocolate shop and gift shop, called contraband.

The Coast display in St Catherine's Quay

More recent additions to Blackgang in 2011, include Fairyland, this enchanting land, has a number of child size fairy houses for children to play inside complete with little chairs and tables. There are fairies and goblins hidden in the trees for you to find, and a toadstool ring to climb on.

Journey into Imagination

The goblins from the Rumpus Mansion gatehouse are also now located in Fairyland, as is the fairy castle.

The fairy houses

Fairyland and the fairy castle

Pirate Cove was created in 2012, here children can become pirates and shoot enemies on the other ship with water cannons.

The two fighting Galleons in Pirate Cove

Galleon in Pirate Cove

Journey into Imagination

In 2013, Blackgang introduced The Dodos. The dodo was a flightless bird native to the island of Mauritius in the Indian Ocean. They were made extinct due to the number of sailors arriving on the island after long voyages and seeking a good meal! The last recorded sighting of a dodo was in 1662.

The Blackgang Dodos are fun animated birds which sing, dance and jump out at the unsuspecting visitor. The story being that pirates left behind dodo eggs, which after being buried for many years, were found by staff when building a new bridge, and to their enormous surprise later hatched into the singing, riotous dodos!

The walkway surrounding the dodos has various buttons to press to provide an interactive experience for the children.

The Dodos

Shadow and Sheila

Shadow and Sheila are life size 'puppet' dinosaurs that perform shows for the public around the park and in an arena. They are baby T-Rex dinosaurs that are under the care of their keepers. In addition some new baby puppet dinosaurs have recently joined the team and have their own puppet show that takes place at various times throughout the year.
Here visitors have the opportunity to pet the dinosaurs and interact with them.

Shadow and the Blackgang dinosaur themed bus

Blackgang launched a new double decker bus at the same time, with the dinosaur design. This coincided with the dinosaur movie 'Walking with Dinosaurs.' which had been partly filmed on the Island and premiered over in Newport.

Journey into Imagination

Sheila in the Shadow and Sheila show

Shadow and Sheila performing

Area 5

The restricted Area 5 allows visitors to experience a whole new dinosaur park. This area opened in 2013; the new animated dinosaurs enable visitors to get a feel of what it would be like if dinosaurs were alive today. The way they are landscaped into the environment gives the dinosaurs a feel that Area 5 is a 'Jurassic Park' on the Isle of Wight. It is a modern version of the dinosaur zoo. At the entrance to Area 5, there is a special IPad app, where you can see yourself alongside dinosaurs, and even take a photo!

T-Rex in Area 5

These dinosaurs are the largest animatronic dinosaurs in Britain. They react to visitors as they walk past, by roaring and moving; one even squirts water!

Journey into Imagination

Water squirting dino!

Entrance to Area 5

Stegosaurus in Area 5

New family of Triceratops for 2015

Journey into Imagination

In addition the Frontierland has been revamped for 2015. A new area with a General Stores has been built, and the Indian Camp moved into its own setting.

Indian Camp

National Bank building with a hold up taking place has also been built, along with a Tabernacle metal chapel, like the one built by the early members of the Dabell family for the local community. There is a network of tunnels for children to explore and they can even try out coffins for size in the undertakers, or create their own 'Wanted' posters.

Bank and Tabernacle

General Stores

Journey into Imagination

Blackgang Events

Over its 170 year history, Blackgang Chine has held numerous events. Here is a selection of just some of the exciting events that have taken place over the decades. In addition, Blackgang has had various characters to entertain park visitors; one of the earliest was Bron the brontosaurus, which was created by David Bellamy in the early 1980s. Bodger The Badger was a well-known character at the park for a few years in the late 1990s, and early 2000s. He was a smuggler badger, and a year later Connie The Fox was introduced as Bodger The Badger's enemy the customs officer. They even had their own show for a few years in the early 2000s written by the Park manager at the time, Simon Dabell, and performed on the Frontierland stage. Today Shadow and Sheila take on the role of visitor entertainment around the park.

Bodger The Badger and Connie The Fox

Isle of Wight Conker Championships

In October 2005, Blackgang Chine held the British Junior Conker Championships. The competitors were banned from bringing their own conkers this year, to avoid them being doctored with varnish or vinegar, or leaving them in a darkened cupboard for a year, which are all traditional ways of creating that winning hardened conker! The competitors had to thread their conkers that were supplied by the park under supervision from stewards. It was hoped that the conker championships would become a nationwide event. The conker game originated in its present form on the Isle of Wight back in 1844, when children were first recorded as playing conkers in Newport. Prior to this, children used to play with snail shells, but once the Horse Chestnut trees arrived from France in the 1830s, conkers became a more popular option. 2001 was the year that Blackgang re-launched the championships which had not been held there since 1996. In 1993, the television presenter Michael Palin was famously disqualified for cheating!
There was also live music at this family event, alongside the peculiar sport of woodlice racing!

Cowboy Hoe downs

These events took place in Frontierland, with lots of country music, food and dancing. There were Western dancing displays, archery and even shoot outs! All ending with an evening barn dance.

Journey into Imagination

Barn dancing at a Wild West Hoe down

Wild West characters taking part in a Hoe down event

150th anniversary events

The celebrations for the 150th anniversary of the park began on 29th March 1993, with a joint celebration alongside the primary school children of Chale, as their school also had its 150th birthday. The children together with the Blackgang team released 150 helium balloons to mark the start of the year's events. A new bus was also painted to commemorate the anniversary.

The release of the 150 balloons

Journey into Imagination

Bodger The Badger and the children of Chale Primary

Other events planned were a Bungy jumping weekend, a conker championship, ghost and ghoul experience and a pirate fiesta.

Pirate Party nights

Pirate themes were popular events in Blackgang's event history, here are details of three very different pirate themed events.
In 1993, a Pirate Fiesta was held. This included a rainbow steel orchestra and a carnival band to produce a Caribbean atmosphere. A Superhero competition was also held to celebrate the parks 150th anniversary. In this event, competitors took part in a re-enactment of a local legend; of the ten brave local heroes who battled against stormy seas to save the crew of the St Mary of Santander. The contest was held to see who would get to keep the silver cutlass that

was found aboard the ship's bounty! There were seven rounds, each depicting a different stage of the legend.

In 1997, Pirate Party nights were held, where children could meet the evil Mick da Silver and his motley crew. They could witness battles between them and the sailor hero Horatio Kneeldown and his beloved Katrina Swashbuckle. These parties included sword fighting, limbo and walking the plank as well as a treasure chest and a hog roast.

Pirates taking part in the Pirate Fiesta

Journey into Imagination

Pirate Crew taking part in the Pirate Party events

Queen Elizabeth diamond jubilee celebrations

In 2012, Pirate Cove opened with the two new pirate ships complete with water cannons and bridges connecting the two. In addition, Blackgang held a pirate jubilee party, with activities centering around Pirate Cove. There were pirates roaming around the park, helping children to find hidden treasure, alongside a BBQ, bands, jugglers and fire eaters. Furthermore, there was a living history team showing visitors how the cannon was loaded, and what life was like back in the days of pirates. A pirate training school was also running.

Alice Tea Party

In 1991, Blackgang held a Mad Hatters Tea Party, of which Alice, the Mad Hatter, Tweedle Dum and Tweedle Dee were present, alongside Sid and Gaffer from Tetley Tea. This A-Maze-ing Tea Party was held to celebrate 1991 as being the year of the maze. This event offered free cups of tea, a fancy dress competition, maze races, live jazz music and an Isle of Wight Radio roadshow.

Alice and the team at the Tea Party

Journey into Imagination

Blackgang Fairy Fling

This event takes place in May and offers visitors the chance to dress as fairy's, join in a fairy dance, and do lots of fairy craft. A dance performance also takes place with fairy dancers performing a story.

Fairies dancing

With wandering wizards doing magic tricks and fairies to meet, visitors could also decorate their own fairy cakes and make a wish to hang on the wishing tree.

There is even the opportunity to make your own fairy potion

Making a potion with a witch!

Blackgang Halloween Restricted Area 5

This event has been going since 2014 with the introduction of the new dinosaurs to the park. Floodlighting has again been added to the park, making it an even more magical experience to visitors. Certain sections of the park are floodlit, and the dinosaurs in Area 5 come to life as night falls. Live actors also add to the eerie atmosphere creating a life like scenario of a real life Jurassic park!

Journey into Imagination

Illuminated Stegosaurus

The T-Rex illuminated for the Halloween event

Conclusion

Over its 170 year history, Blackgang Chine has gone from a natural landscape of gardens, the business being set up by Alexander Dabell; to a theme park containing rides and attractions managed by the latest in a long line of Dabells, Alexander Dabell. Through changing tastes and attitudes, the park has evolved to suit the tourist industry, as Victorian, pre and post war work patterns and conceptions of entertainment changed over time. The park maintained its appeal by keeping the old favorites, yet still kept up to date by adding something new each year. The whimsical tableaux enable visitors to create their own story with their imagination, providing an educational and enriching experience. Where else can you play amongst dinosaurs, be a fairy, battle pirates and take part in a shoot-out in cowboy terrain all in the same day?

As the park has moved increasingly eastwards and upwards over the years, due to the substantial amounts of land that have been lost from erosion. The landscape has undoubtedly changed, yet with the re-siting of many popular attractions Blackgang has kept its old worldly charm, to draw the older visitor and keep nostalgia alive. Furthermore, by investing in the latest technological attractions, Blackgang has appealed to the younger visitor aswell, as the old. Making it a unique attraction, and the oldest theme park in the UK.

Journey into Imagination

Printed in Great Britain
by Amazon